BLOODSUCKING
C R E A T U R E S

Bizarre Science

Ron Knapp

Enslow Publishers, Inc.
40 Industrial Road
Box 398
Berkeley Heights, NJ 07922
USA

http://www.enslow.com

Original edition published as *Bloodsuckers* in 1996.

Library of Congress Cataloging-in-Publication Data

Knapp, Ron.
  Bloodsucking creatures / Ron Knapp.
    p. cm. — (Bizarre science)
  Summary: "Examines animals that feed on blood, including mosquitoes, vampire bats, lice, leeches, lampreys, and fleas, and looks at their anatomy, behavior, and interactions with people"— Provided by publisher.
  Includes bibliographical references and index.
  ISBN 978-0-7660-3671-0
  1. Bloodsucking animals—Juvenile literature. I. Title.
  QL756.55.K584 2011
  591.5'3—dc22
                    2010009761

Paperback ISBN 978-1-59845-219-8

Printed in the United States of America

102010 Lake Book Manufacturing, Inc., Melrose Park, IL

10 9 8 7 6 5 4 3 2 1

To Our Readers:
We have done our best to make sure all Internet addresses in this book were active and appropriate when we went to press. However, the author and the publisher have no control over and assume no liability for the material available on those Internet sites or on other Web sites they may link to. Any comments or suggestions can be sent by e-mail to comments@enslow.com or to the address on the back cover.

♻ Enslow Publishers, Inc., is committed to printing our books on recycled paper. The paper in every book contains 10% to 30% post-consumer waste (PCW). The cover board on the outside of each book contains 100% PCW. Our goal is to do our part to help young people and the environment too!

Illustration Credits: The Art Archive / Bibliothèque Nationale Paris, p. 35; © blickwinkel / Alamy, pp. 21, 29, 40; Everett Collection, p. 16; Jacana / Photo Researchers, Inc., p. 27; Janice Haney Carr / Public Health Image Library / CDC, p. 30; © Jim Clare / npl / Minden Pictures, p. 15; © Kevin Dyer / istockphoto.com, p. 22; Martin Dohrn / Photo Researchers, Inc., p. 42; © Michael and Patricia Fogden / Minden Pictures, p. 1; Peter Arnold Images / Photolibrary, pp. 7, 12; Public Health Image Library / CDC, p. 33; Shutterstock.com, pp. 4, 10, 32, 36, 38, 44; Superstock / Photolibrary, p. 14; SPL / Photo Researchers, Inc., p. 18; U.S. Fish and Wildlife Service, p. 24; © WildPictures / Alamy, p. 9.

Cover Illustration: © Michael and Patricia Fogden / Minden Pictures (A vampire bat in Costa Rica).

CONTENTS

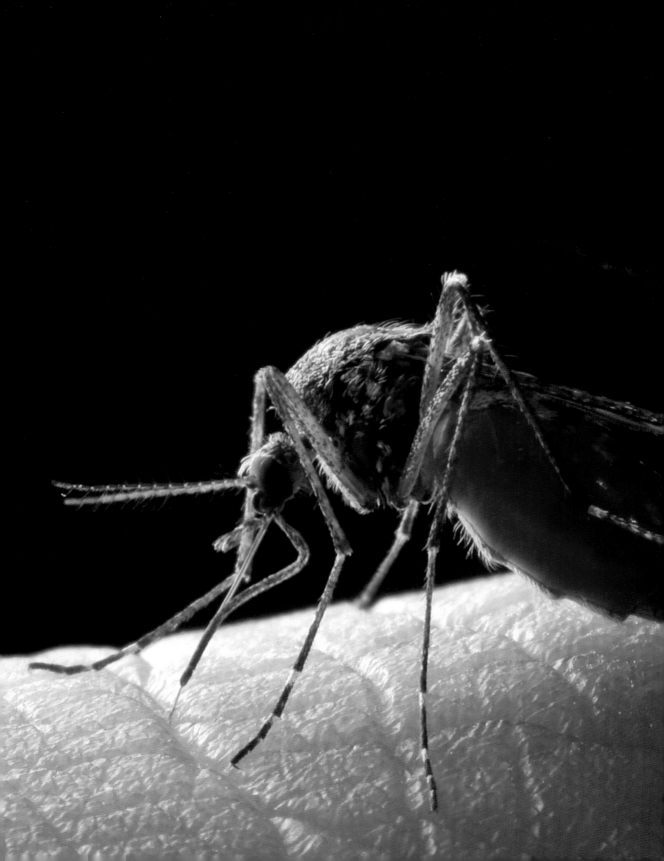

Mosquitoes

One of the world's smallest animals is one of the most dangerous. Throughout the ages, mosquitoes have caused the deaths of millions of people. They are so light, though, that it would take 300,000 of them to weigh as much as a can of soda pop.

An adult mosquito gets nourishment by sucking through its proboscis, the long sharp "drill" that sticks out of its mouth. It stays alive by sucking the nectar out of flowers.

Flying from flower to flower, the female mosquito sounds like a tiny engine. Her wings beat almost five hundred times a second, making a weird buzzing sound. That's her way of getting the attention of the male mosquitoes. The males flock around a female as soon as they hear her buzzing. She mates with one, then flies away with the male's sperm stored in her body.

A mosquito fills up on blood by sucking through its proboscis.

After that, her mate has nothing left to do. Within two weeks, he's dead. The female lives much longer. She has an important job to do. Hundreds of eggs begin to grow inside her body. She needs to nourish them, but nectar won't help. It is mostly made of sugar. The only food that will make the eggs grow properly is animal blood.

They Want You

One of the best sources of blood is human beings. Mosquitoes can find you—even in the dark—because their antennae sense the chemicals given off by your body. They drill into your skin and suck out your blood. The proboscis of the female is covered with sharp, jagged stylets. They pump up and down furiously as she jabs her proboscis into your skin. Once inside, she bends it back and forth, looking under your skin for a tiny blood tube called a capillary.

When she finds blood with her proboscis, the female pours saliva into your body. It thins your blood so that it is easier for her to suck. Then she pumps the blood through a small tube in her proboscis. It only takes about ninety seconds for her to fill her abdomen with blood. By then she's dark and swollen.

After she is finished, the female pulls her proboscis out of your skin and flies away. For the next few days she rests, allowing her body to digest its bloody meal. The eggs grow, and soon she lays them in water.

Itchy Bites

But what about you? Usually you do not even notice being bitten. You are so much larger than a mosquito that you don't miss the tiny amount of blood sucked out of your body. What you do notice is the swelling around the bite. The mosquito's saliva irritates your skin. Blood rushes to the area of the bite, and a small bump forms. For a while, it itches.

If itchy little bumps were the only problems caused by mosquitoes, scientists and doctors would not worry about them.

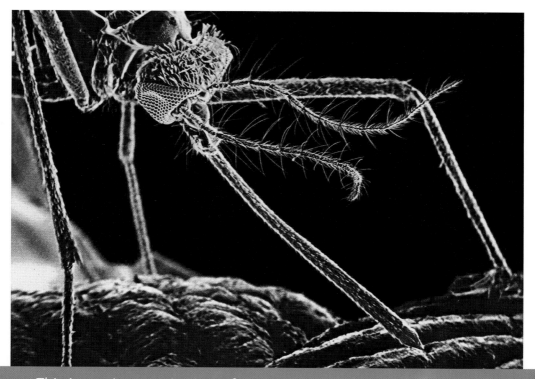

This is a microscopic view of a mosquito drilling its proboscis into human skin. Mosquitoes release saliva into your blood to keep it flowing when they feast on you.

But sometimes, mosquitoes spread diseases. When a female squirts her saliva into a victim, it can be full of germs taken from a person or an animal bitten a few minutes earlier. The germs get into the new victim's body and can cause serious diseases like yellow fever, malaria, and encephalitis.

Gorgas Saves the Canal

About a hundred years ago, mosquitoes almost prevented the building of the Panama Canal. French companies wanted to dig the canal through the jungles of Panama to connect the Atlantic and Pacific oceans. It was a hot, swampy area—a perfect spot for mosquitoes to lay their eggs. The female mosquitoes feasted on the blood of thousands of workers. Soon, the workmen began dying from malaria and yellow fever. Finally, the French gave up and went home.

That's when William Gorgas, an American sanitation expert, went to work. He drained swamps around the route of the canal so the mosquitoes would not have a place to lay their eggs. He sprayed oil and insecticides to kill the pesky insects. He put screens on windows and covered beds with mosquito netting. Soon, the workers were safe, and the canal was completed.

Chemicals Don't Work

Today, modern medicines have just about wiped out most of the diseases carried by mosquitoes in the United States, but the insects are still a nuisance. In the 1940s and 1950s, scientists

Female mosquitoes like to lay their eggs in standing water. Here, some newborn larvae come out of the eggs.

thought they had the answer: a chemical called DDT, which is an insecticide that kills almost all mosquitoes. Thousands of acres were sprayed. The mosquito problem was almost solved, but a brand-new problem was created when a few of the mosquitoes survived. They were immune to DDT, and the chemical did not bother them at all. The mosquitoes that hatched from their eggs were immune, too. It took stronger and stronger doses of DDT and other poisons to kill them. But those chemicals also killed wildlife and made many people sick. The use of DDT was stopped in the United States in the early 1970s.

The Fight Goes On

Today, scientists have many ways to control insects and don't rely solely on insect poisons. These scientists are experimenting with chemical traps that attract mosquitoes but do not bother anything else.[1] They also use animals like bats that love to eat mosquitoes. Scientists are looking for species of insects that could eat mosquito larvae and for tiny wasps that eat mosquito eggs.

You, too, can help fight mosquitoes. Make sure your family does not leave standing water around your house. Thousands of

A lodge house in the Amazon region of South America has mosquito nets hung over the beds. This is a good way to protect people from mosquitoes in the regions where the insects could be carrying dangerous diseases.

eggs can be laid in a soggy ditch or an old barrel filled with water. Spraying mosquito repellent on your skin will not kill the bugs, but it will keep them away from you. The repellent works by preventing mosquitoes from noticing the heat and moisture given off by your body. They cannot "see" you with their antennae, so they leave you alone.

They're Here to Stay

It is estimated that there are 100 trillion mosquitoes in the world today. That is about 20,000 for every person on the planet. Each day about 33 trillion—or one-third—of the mosquitoes die. Some are swatted and squashed by irritated humans, but most are eaten by bats, lizards, birds, and spiders. The mosquitoes are an important part of their diet. If the tiny bloodsucking insects disappeared, the animals that eat them would be in trouble. Luckily for the bats, lizards, birds, and spiders, all the mosquitoes that die are quickly replaced by trillions more that hatch.

Mosquitoes can be controlled but probably never eliminated. After all, they have been around a long, long time. Millions of years before the first humans, they were already here, sucking the blood out of dinosaurs.

Vampire Bats

Vampires are real, but you won't find them sleeping in coffins or hanging around dark, gloomy castles. They're usually hanging upside down in caves. Vampires are not tall, spooky men dressed in black. They are reddish-brown and are only about three inches long. Real vampires are bats!

They may not be as creepy looking as Count Dracula or the other fictional vampires you see in movies, but they are certainly ugly. Up close, a vampire bat looks like a cross between a mouse and a spider. It has pointed claws, big ears, a stubby nose, two razor-sharp teeth, and a bright red tongue.

Busy at Night

Like most other bats, vampires are nocturnal, which means they sleep through the day so they can be active at night. Their schedule works out well, because they can only get their nourishment

A group of vampire bats hang upside down in their cave home in Argentina.

A vampire bat flies out from its home in search of a meal. Cattle, pigs, goats, and birds are typical victims of vampire bats.

when their victims are sleeping. No animal that is awake and alert would let a vampire bat get anywhere near it.

When the sun goes down, the bats get busy. They fly out of their caves looking for a meal. Vampires think cattle blood is very tasty. They also like blood from pigs, goats, and birds. Sometimes, they will even land on a human and start sucking. They're not fussy. If an animal has blood, it is a possible victim.

Dogs are one of the few types of animals that are not bothered much by vampires. That's because dogs hear so well. Vampires make a high-pitched screeching sound when they fly. Dogs hear the noise and wake up. If an animal is awake, the vampire will fly right by.

The Silent Slurping Attack

Once a vampire bat finds a suitable victim, it lands nearby, usually on the ground. Then it tucks its big, thin wings under its body and closes in. Hopping and creeping silently on its clawed feet, the bat looks for the best place to strike. Since the vampire bat is so light, the sleeping victim usually does not even notice the footsteps up its leg or across its back.

Soon, the bat has picked its spot. It quickly sinks a pair of tiny, triangular teeth into the flesh of its victim. On cattle, the neck is the best place to strike. The skin is soft there and filled with veins and arteries. A lot of blood can also be found in the nose of a pig or the ear of a goat. On humans, the best spots are fingers, toes, lips, and the forehead.

No matter the spot, and regardless of the type of animal, the result is the same. Once the teeth are removed from the tiny wound, the victim begins to bleed. The bat's saliva keeps the blood from clotting into a scab. Now it's feeding time!

So that it does not miss a drop, the bat curls its tongue into a funnel. The blood travels through the tongue, into the mouth, down the esophagus, and into the stomach. A vampire bat's digestive system cannot handle solid foods. Blood is the only thing that can keep it alive.

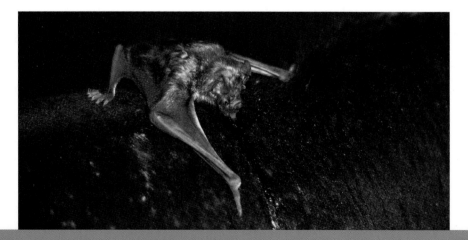

A vampire bat feeds on cattle blood. Vampire bats curl their tongues into a funnel to suck up as much blood as possible.

While it's slurping, the bat keeps very quiet and still. It wants its victim to stay asleep so that the meal can continue. After about half an hour of slurping, the vampire has to stop. Its stomach is so full, it can barely fly back to its cave. When it finally gets there, it falls asleep and lets its body digest the blood.

Meanwhile, the victim is probably still asleep. Usually, the wound bleeds a little bit after the bat leaves. Human victims might notice a little blood on their bedclothes when they wake up, but they will probably have trouble finding the wound. Vampires don't leave much of a trace. Their bite is only about a tenth of an inch wide. You can get much worse cuts from bumping into a door or falling off your bike. Human victims will probably never miss the blood stolen during the night. Since vampires are so tiny, birds are usually the only animals they can bleed to death.

Sometimes, a vampire cannot find a meal before it returns to its cave. But it doesn't need to go hungry if it has good friends to rely on. Vampire bats can recognize each other and will ask another bat to share its blood meal, which it can regurgitate into its friend's mouth. Next time, their roles may be reversed and the favor is paid back. The bats can remember who shared with them in the past. They are willing to share with the bats who helped them out when they needed it.

Vampires Aren't Human

For humans and most animals, the problem with vampire bats is not the blood they take, but the microorganisms they leave behind. The teeth and saliva of the bats often carry bacteria and viruses that cause dangerous infections. Some of their victims get rabies, a disease that destroys nerve cells in the brain. If left untreated and without proper medication, death will result.

For centuries, people in Europe have told frightening stories about human vampires who must suck the blood of other humans to stay alive. Supposedly, a vampire is very tough to kill—you have to put a stake through its heart. The people of Europe need not worry, because, of course, there have never been any human vampires. Today, there are no real vampire bats living there—or in the United States, either. The bats living in Europe and the United States are not interested in blood. Their idea of a good mealtime is a night spent eating insects.

The world's only real bloodsucking bats live in Central and South America and on a few Caribbean islands. Most of the time, they do not bother humans. It's a lot easier to get the blood they need from cattle or other farm animals.

This magnified color scan of a head louse shows its claws clinging to a strand of human hair.

Head Lice

Head lice are not dangerous. They are pesky nuisances. They don't just want to suck your blood. They want to move in and turn the forest of hair on your head into their home.

A louse is only about a tenth of an inch long, and it is usually very pale, almost transparent. It would be hard to spot no matter where it was, but it's even tougher to see because it likes to hide under thick patches of hair. Unless you are using a magnifying glass, it is almost impossible to spot one on somebody's head. So if you have head lice, you probably will not notice them until you feel what they are doing to your head.

To stay alive, a louse needs to suck human blood. The head, of course, is a perfect spot. The insect can stay warm and hidden in the hair. Since the part of the head under the skin is covered by capillaries, the louse always has plenty of food.

Claws and Teeth

A louse's body is very simple and efficient. The curved claws on its six legs are designed to grasp hold of hairs so that the insect can have a firm grip while it goes to work. The louse uses tiny teeth to bite into the skin of the scalp. Then it drops a long beak into the fresh wound. Soon, it is sucking blood right out of the victim's head.

The person usually does not feel the louse's bite or the blood being sucked out. The louse is free to drink until it is full. By then, it is no longer pale. Its color is dark red from all the blood it has swallowed.

The Lice Multiply

One louse will not cause much of a problem, but most people do not have just one louse for long. One female can lay as many as ten eggs a day.[1] She glues her white eggs one at a time to single strands of hair. The eggs, or nits as they are sometimes called, are easier to spot than the lice themselves. They look like dandruff or pieces of light-colored dust, but they cannot be brushed off or blown away like dandruff. They are stuck securely to the hairs.

If the eggs are not removed, they will hatch in about ten days. The new lice lay more eggs. Soon, the person's head becomes the home of a community of the pests. They do not suck enough blood to cause the person serious harm, and they do not carry any dangerous diseases, but their bites soon begin to itch. For many people, the first indication of head lice comes when they notice

Head lice use their claws to move along the hairs on a person's head and use their tiny teeth to bite into the scalp for their blood meal.

how much they are scratching their heads. The itchiest spots are usually behind the ears and on the back of the head. There, the hair is thickest, and the lice have more places to hide.[2]

once You've Got Them . . .

Scratching will not get rid of the nasty pests. Neither will regular soap or shampoo. A good hard shower might knock many of the insects off the head, but it will not bother most of the nits.

Head lice, especially nits, cannot be removed from hair with regular shampoo or a standard comb. In this photo, a mother grooms her son of head lice with a special nit comb.

They will remain stuck to the hairs until new lice hatch out and replace the ones that were washed away.

The only way to make sure all the lice are gone is to use a special shampoo designed to kill all the lice and the nits. Some doctors also recommend using a special comb that will be sure to remove all the nits from the hair.

However, washing and combing are often not enough, even with special shampoos and combs. Sometimes lice are accidentally knocked off onto combs, brushes, towels, sheets, blankets, or clothing. From there, they can find their way right back onto a head that has just been cleaned. The problem begins all over again. Any household item that came in contact with the hair must be thoroughly cleaned.

It is a lot harder to get rid of lice than it is to stay away from them in the first place. Health officials advise people not to share combs, hats, and scarves. If students are not careful, lice can spread to a whole classroom in just a few weeks. Soon, everybody is itching!

A close-up image of the mouth of a lamprey.

Lampreys

The ancient Romans noticed a very odd animal swimming upstream through their rivers. It looked like a fat, king-sized worm. Every now and then it stopped to suck on a stone stuck into the bank. Sometimes it pulled small stones off the bottom of the stream and swam away with them. The Romans named the strange creature "lamprey," or "stone-sucker."

Holding on With Their Mouths

Scientists later figured out that lampreys anchor themselves with their mouths onto big rocks so that they can rest. It's not easy swimming against the current, but that's what they have to do on their way to spawn, or lay eggs. Prior to spawning, the male makes a nest from a pile of little stones.

When the nest is completed, the male uses his sucker to anchor himself to the female. Then he wraps his body around her, squeezing tightly so that thousands of eggs are pushed out of her body. As the eggs fall into the nest, he fertilizes them with his sperm. Soon, both parents are dead, exhausted from the long trip upstream and the laying of the eggs.

Hiding in the Sand

When the offspring hatch, they are on their own. At first, they don't look much like their parents. They appear to be tiny, transparent worms. To hide from predators, they burrow into the soft sand of the streambed. Only their big mouths stick out of the sand, catching small organisms. As the lampreys grow, their slimy skin turns tan or brown. They continue to hide in the sand until they're fully grown. Sometimes that takes as long as seven years. Different types of lampreys range in size from a few inches to three feet long.

Patient and Deadly

A lamprey is a perfectly designed sucking machine. Its round mouth can easily attach to almost any surface. Lampreys do not just suck stones or hold on to other lampreys. When they are fully grown, they stop eating organisms that happen to swim into their mouths. As adults, they become deadly bloodsuckers.

Their victims are almost always fish. Lampreys rarely attack people. They keep away from the warmth of the human body. That's lucky for us, since these bloodsuckers usually hang on to their victims for long periods of time. Tiny teeth on the inside of

This sea lamprey preys on a smaller fish. Lampreys' victims are usually fish or whales, and they almost never attack humans.

the lamprey's mouth dig into the scales of the unlucky fish. They are almost impossible to shake off.

Have you ever heard of a tongue with teeth? That's what does most of the work for the lamprey. Scientists call the extra teeth "dental plates." They are so jagged and sharp that the lamprey can open a large wound just by scraping its tongue back and forth. Then the sucking begins. To make the job easier, the lamprey injects a powerful chemical into its victims. Not only does this chemical stop the blood from clotting, but it also dissolves the tissues around the wound.

A lamprey is patient. It will keep sucking for four or five hours. If its victim is a small fish, the lamprey will usually suck it dry, and the animal will not be released until it is dead. On a larger fish or a whale, the lamprey will suck on one spot for a while, then move to another part of the same body. After a while, it moves on to another victim before it has sucked all the blood out of a large animal. That fortunate survivor is easy to spot. For the rest of its life, it will bear a round scar from the attack.

Stopped by TFM

Even if they do not like the taste of humans, lampreys have caused plenty of other kinds of trouble for them. For centuries, sea lampreys could not move into the Great Lakes from the Atlantic Ocean because they were stopped by Niagara Falls. Then the Welland Canal and St. Lawrence Seaway were built to connect the Great Lakes to the Atlantic Ocean. Lampreys found they could use the canal as easily as the ships could. Soon, they had made their way into all the Great Lakes, where they feasted on the blood of millions of fish. Soon, many types of fish began to disappear. Fishermen feared there would be nothing left in the Great Lakes except lampreys.[1] Miles of nets were strung up to catch the bloodsuckers. Even electric fences were built across streams. Nothing worked until scientists tried a chemical called TFM, which killed lampreys but did not seem to harm any other fish. Soon, the lamprey population in the Great Lakes began to fall.

Lampreys swim against the current to spawn, or lay eggs.
To rest, they use their mouths to grip a stone, like this
European river lamprey.

Fish and wildlife agencies then restocked the lake with trout and coho salmon, a non-native species in the Great Lakes region.[2]

When they are under control, lampreys also have a positive role to play in the environment. They serve as food for many larger fish and birds, and, believe it or not, lampreys used to be a very popular food for humans! In parts of New England, people loved the taste of lampreys that had been seasoned in smoke-houses. However, in more recent years, hardly anybody has had the stomach to eat this creature.

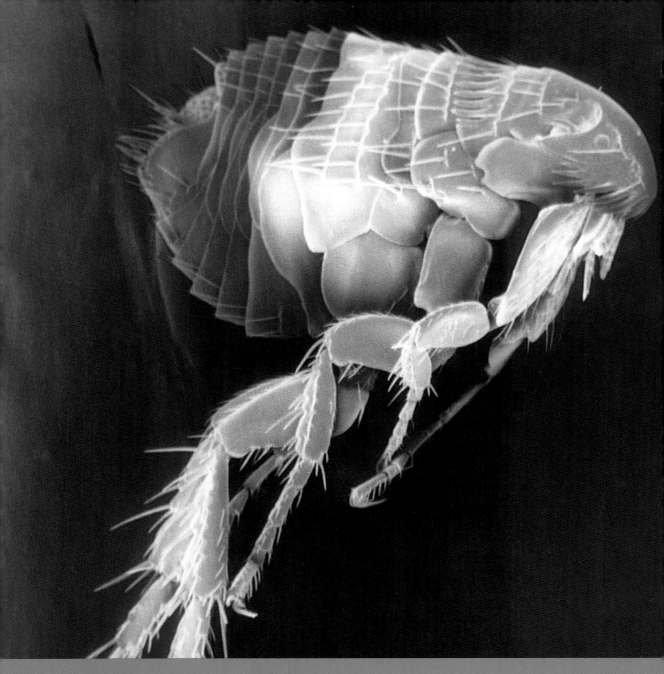

A magnified view of a flea. Fleas, although they are tiny insects, caused major problems in Europe during the Middle Ages.

Fleas

For centuries, the most dangerous animal in the world was the flea. It killed more people than all the wars of the Middle Ages. During one epidemic, almost a third of the people living in Europe died.

Of course, the fleas did not know that they were killers. All they wanted was a little blood. It didn't matter if it came from dogs or cats or people. The problem with fleas was that they also liked rat blood. During the Middle Ages, most cities had huge populations of rats. These pesky rodents also lived in ships that traveled from country to country. Unfortunately, some of those rats were infected by a terrible disease called the plague.

Living on Rats

Rats are a fine home for fleas. Their hairs provide a good place to hide. Since fleas are tiny, flat insects, it is very easy for them to crawl between hairs. They're covered with shiny plates that make them very hard. They're almost impossible to squish. When a flea is hungry, it just sinks its sharp proboscis into the rat's skin. Then the flea sticks a pair of pumping tubes from its mouth into the victim. One sucks up the blood, while the other pumps saliva into the wound. The saliva contains a chemical that prevents clotting. It will also make the wound itch when the flea is done.

Spreading the Plague

Fleas became killers by sucking the blood of the plague-infected rats. Eventually, the rats would die, and the fleas would move on to a new victim, usually other rats. Even though they do not have

Fleas like to hide in the hairs of rats and drink their blood. In the Middle Ages, fleas spread the plague by drinking the blood of infected rats and then passing it on to humans.

This is a diagram of a flea. Although fleas do not have wings, they can move easily by jumping with their strong hind legs.

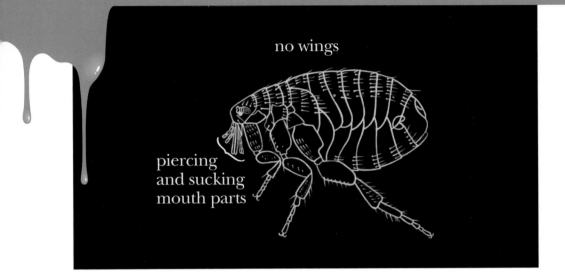

no wings

piercing
and sucking
mouth parts

wings, fleas have no trouble moving. With their strong hind legs, they can jump as far as thirteen inches.

The blood of the sick rats infected the fleas, too. The germs in the fleas' blood multiplied quickly in the insects' intestines. Soon, their clogged intestines made it impossible for the fleas to digest any blood.

In a desperate attempt to stay alive, the fleas kept sucking blood from their new victims, but there was no place to put it. The fleas spit up germs into the fresh wound. Soon, the infected fleas were dead. However, they had already passed on the disease. More fleas hatched and took their place.

Sometimes when a rat died, its fleas would move onto the body of a nearby human being. Soon, the person was infected by the vomit of the sick insects. Within a few days, the person had the plague. At first, the person just felt weak and uncomfortable. Then parts of his or her body began to swell, and purple blotches appeared on the skin. The person's heart beat faster and faster, trying to get blood through the swollen tissues. After about five days, the pain became very intense. The sufferer began to scream and beg for mercy. Finally, the person lost control of his or her muscles and made strange, jerky movements. After that, the victim of the horrible disease finally died.

Soon, the streets were filled with the rotting bodies of plague victims. Everybody was terrified. They wanted to make sure they did not get the disease themselves. But they did not understand how it was spread, so they did some things that seem strange to us. They tried to avoid the plague by chanting magic spells to fight off the evil spirits they thought had brought the disease.[1] They blamed people with different religions for bringing the disease into their town, so they burned down their places of worship and killed them. If somebody in a family got the plague, sometimes their home was walled up—with the uninfected members still inside—so that the disease could not "get out." One general turned the plague into a weapon. He put dead, infected bodies on catapults and flung them into his enemy's camps.[2]

Nobody suspected that the cause of all this horror was the pesky little fleas. Back then, the tiny pests were a normal part of

This French painting from around 1503 shows Death taking plague victims. The plague killed at least one-third of Europe's population during the outbreak in the 1300s.

Today, the main victims of fleas are our household pets. Dogs and cats will scratch hard to get rid of them. This puppy gives his furry coat a good scratch.

everyday life. Everybody had them, since hardly anybody ever took baths and most people did not think of changing clothes. Rich women wore fancy flea traps, but they were not very effective. One of Sweden's queens even tried to get rid of her fleas by shooting them with a tiny crossbow. While they were scratching all their flea bites, nobody in the Middle Ages realized that those tiny insects were killing them.

Still Dangerous

Luckily for us, modern cities have gotten rid of millions of rats. There are still plenty of fleas, but they can be controlled by chemicals. Scientists have also developed new medicines that help prevent the plague from breaking out again.

Fleas are not much of a problem in the United States today. We change our clothes regularly, so they can't hide there or lay their eggs in the seams. A good hot shower can usually send most fleas on their way. Probably the most effective weapon against them is the vacuum cleaner. Fleas love to lay eggs in thick, lush carpeting. Vacuum cleaners can easily suck them all up before they hatch.

Today, when we think of fleas, we mostly worry about the pain they cause our pets. Cats and dogs are the main victims now. Even when fleas do not carry dangerous diseases, their bites still itch. Animals scratch very hard to get rid of them. Sometimes they make themselves bleed. Veterinarians recommend sprays, special shampoos, and even flea collars to get rid of the pests. Since they sometimes nest in the area where a pet sleeps, it's also a good idea to change the bedding regularly.

Other parts of the world are not so lucky. In September 1993, an earthquake drove a large population of rats from the jungle near Bid, India. Soon the rats—and their fleas—came in contact with people. Less than a year later, hundreds of the people had the plague.[3] Once again, fleas had transferred the terrible disease from the rats to human beings, and the world was reminded that fleas can be killers.

A leech takes hold of a person's skin, preparing to suck some blood.

Leeches

People have used leeches for thousands of years. In ancient times, when children were bitten by insects or even poisonous snakes, the best "medicine" their parents had was often one of these slimy little worms. The leech would be placed on the bite and left alone. With any luck, it would suck the poison or irritating bit of bug saliva right out of the body. Sometimes it worked, and the child felt better.

Three Jaws and a Pair of Suckers

There are many kinds of leeches. They range in length from half an inch to almost twelve inches. Their bodies have two suckers, a big one at the bottom and a smaller one at the head. They use the suckers to get a grip on the surface beneath them so that they can move quickly. The suckers also come in handy when the

A leech has three sharp jaws, pictured here, that allow it to cut through the skin to suck up blood. Then a leech injects a chemical called, hirudin, to prevent the blood from clotting.

leech wants to drink some blood. Each worm has both male and female parts. When a pair of them mate, they are fertilizing each other's eggs.

When a leech is firmly attached to another animal, it slices through the skin with its three sharp jaws. At the same time, it injects a painkilling chemical into the wound so that the victim feels nothing. Another chemical, hirudin, prevents the blood from clotting. Then the leech is free to suck up its meal.

Many different types of leeches are found in jungles, marshes, and other wetland areas around the world. They usually find their own food by attaching to the bodies of humans and animals that pass through their habitats. If you ever find a leech stuck to your skin, don't panic. They hardly ever carry any diseases. Just grab hold of it and pull. Their suckers are not strong enough to hold them on too tightly.

"Bad Blood"

During the Middle Ages, leeches almost disappeared from some parts of the world. They were constantly being hunted so they could be used by doctors. Leeches seemed to be the solution to almost every problem. An overweight patient? Slap on a few leeches and he would lose some weight. A sick, tired patient? No problem. Slap on some more leeches. They would suck out all the "bad blood" that was causing the sickness. Soon, the patient would be as good as new. To speed up the cure, sometimes as many as fifty of the worms were set all over the patient's body.

In the Middle Ages, doctors used leeches to suck out the "bad blood" of a sick person. Doctors discovered that this did more harm than good to a patient. However, today, doctors use medicinal leeches for other healing purposes.

The trouble was that "bad blood" does not cause diseases. The worst thing to do for a weakened patient is to remove blood. That just causes the person more weakness, and sometimes even death. When doctors discovered that germs caused diseases, they quit paying attention to leeches. For decades, the use of leeches to help patients was ridiculed by the medical profession.

A Little Boy Gets Back His Ear

In recent years, however, the medical profession has been giving the worms a second look. In 1985, for instance, a dog in Medford, Massachusetts, attacked five-year-old Guy Condelli and bit off his right ear. Dr. Joseph Upton reattached the ear in a ten-hour operation. But right away there were problems. Before the veins inside could heal, they filled with blood and turned the ear purple. Once the blood was stuck in the veins, there was no way the veins could ever heal. It looked like young Guy would still lose his ear after all.

But then Dr. Upton had an idea. Why not use leeches to drain the excess blood? A company in Wales agreed to fly thirty "medicinal leeches" from London, England, to Massachusetts. Dr. Upton picked up the worms and used eight of them on the boy's ear. Immediately, they began sucking up the excess blood and allowed the ear to heal. A few days later, Guy went home with his ear intact.[1]

Today, some scientists feel leeches can do more than just reduce swelling. They are studying the use of hirudin, the chemical released by leeches. It seems to be much more effective than other chemicals in thinning human blood. People suffering from heart attacks and other heart problems often take medicine to thin their blood. Thin blood does not clot in the arteries, so the patients have fewer heart attacks. Scientists have begun experimenting with hirudin to see if it can do the job better than most traditional medicines.[2]

Leeches have already saved one little boy's ear. Maybe someday, they could save your life.

CHAPTER NOTES

Chapter 1. Mosquitoes

1. Hendrik Hertzberg, "Summer's Blood," *Time*, vol. 140, issue 6, August 10, 1992, p. 48.

Chapter 3. Head Lice

1. Lennie Copeland, *The Lice-Buster Book: What to Do When Your Child Comes Home With Head Lice* (Mill Valley, Calif.: Authentic Pictures, 1995), p. 15.
2. "Questions & Answers about Head Lice," Michigan Department of Public Health booklet.

Chapter 4. Lampreys

1. "Lamprey Control," *Detroit Free Press*, August 7, 1994, p. 2F.
2. Interview with Bill Gruhn, fisheries biologist, Michigan Department of Natural Resources, August 9, 1995.

Chapter 5. Fleas

1. Geddes Smith, *Plague on US* (New York: The Commonwealth Fund, 1941), p. 35.
2. Charles L. Mee, Jr., "How a Mysterious Disease Laid Low Europe's Masses," *Smithsonian*, vol. 20, issue 11, February 1990, p. 69.
3. Tom Post, "The Plague of Panic," *Newsweek*, October 10, 1994, pp. 40–41.

Chapter 6. Leeches

1. Richard Conniff, "The Little Suckers Have Made A Comeback," *Discover*, vol. 8, issue 8, August 1987, pp. 85–86.
2. Kathy A. Fackelmann, "Bloodsuckers Reconsidered: Leech Saliva Inspires a Medical Quest," *Science News*, vol. 139, issue 11, March 16, 1991, p. 172.

GLOSSARY

antennae—The sensory organs that grow from the head of invertebrate (having no backbone) animals.

arteries—Blood vessels that carry blood *away* from the heart.

bacteria—A group of mostly single-celled organisms, identified by their lack of a cell nucleus.

capillary—Tiny microscopic blood vessels in the body. Capillaries ultimately lead from arteries to veins.

clotting—The ability to stop bleeding. Tiny blood cells called platelets stop the flow of blood at wound sites in healthy animals.

DDT—An insect-killer (dichloro-diphenyltrichloroethane) that was widely used in the United States, but later banned. The poison nearly killed off many species of birds.

encephalitis—Swelling of the brain, some-times caused by bacterial or viral infections.

epidemic—A disease that has spread to many people.

esophagus—The tube leading from the mouth to the stomach in most animals.

hirudin—The substance secreted by leeches that thins the blood of their prey, preventing the blood from clotting.

immunity—Resistance to a disease or a poisonous substance.

insecticides—Poisonous chemicals used to kill insects.

invertebrates—A group of animals, including insects, mollusks, and worms, that do not have backbones.

larvae—The tiny wormlike young of insects.

malaria—A sometimes fatal disease of humans, often carried by mosquitoes in tropical regions.

microorganisms—Tiny single-celled organisms invisible to the naked eye.

nits—The eggs of lice.

nocturnal—A creature that is most active at night.

plague—An epidemic where the rate of death is very high.

predators—Animals that hunt down and feed on other animals.

proboscis—In invertebrate animals, the tube extending from the mouth that is used for sucking blood or nectar.

rabies—An often fatal disease of the nervous system. The virus causing the disease is often transmitted through a bite.

regurgitate—To eject, or throw up, what was previously swallowed.

sanitation—The disposal of waste materials.

spawn—The fertilization of a mass of eggs released in water.

stylets—Tubelike, sucking mouthparts in bloodsucking insects.

TFM—A chemical used by scientists to kill lampreys in the Great Lakes.

veins—Blood vessels that carry blood *to* the heart.

virus—The causes of many human and animal diseases, viruses are made of tiny pieces of genetic material. They must use the cells of other organisms to reproduce, and they destroy their host cell.

FURTHER READING

Books

Artell, Mike. *Backyard Bloodsuckers: Questions, Facts & Tongue Twisters About Creepy, Crawly Creatures.* Tucson, Ariz.: Good Year Books, 2008.

DiConsiglio, John. *Blood Suckers!: Deadly Mosquito Bites.* New York: Franklin Watts, 2008.

Houghton, Sarah. *Bloodsuckers: Bats, Bugs, and Other Bloodthirsty Creatures.* Bloomington, Minn.: Red Brick Learning, 2004.

Kite, L. Patricia. *Leeches.* Minneapolis, Minn.: Lerner Publications Co., 2005.

Royston, Angela. *Head Lice.* Mankato, Minn.: Black Rabbit Books, 2009.

Taschek, Karen. *Hanging With Bats: Ecobats, Vampires, and Movie Stars.* Albuquerque, N.M.: University of New Mexico Press, 2008.

Internet Addresses

Mosquitoes, Mosquito Pictures, Mosquito Facts: National Geographic
<http://animals.nationalgeographic.com/animals/bugs/mosquito.html>

PBS: NATURE, Bloody Suckers, Once Bitten
<http://www.pbs.org/wnet/nature/bloodysuckers/interview.html>

Vampire Bat: The Wild Ones
<http://www.thewildones.org/Animals/vampire.html>

INDEX